The RICH FOOL

ARCH Books

© 1964 CONCORDIA PUBLISHING HOUSE, ST. LOUIS, MISSOURI

LIBRARY OF CONGRESS CATALOG CARD NO. 64-16984
MANUFACTURED IN THE UNITED STATES OF AMERICA
ISBN 0-570-06004-4

The RICH FOOL

Written by Janice Kramer
Illustrated by Sally Mathews

LUKE 12:16-21 FOR CHILDREN

A long time ago, in a land far away,
there lived a rich man who did nothing all day
but to think and to worry, to hope and to plan
some way of becoming a wealthier man.

From his house to his fields
each day he would walk
to look at his crops —
every leaf, every stalk.
Then he'd climb to the top
of his great storage bin
where he kept all his grain,
and he'd sit there and grin.

He watched as his slaves labored hard in the sun
to put grain in the bin, loading ton after ton.

As he carefully counted the loads as they came,
he would think of his riches,
his wealth, and his fame.

A few hungry birds in the skies overhead
saw the big bin of grain, and downward they sped.
Oh, how happy they were!
For at last they could eat.
They landed and started to dine on the wheat.

But when the rich man saw them eating his grain,
he screamed and he kicked and waved his big cane.
"You can't have what's mine!
Get away from my bin,
or I'll hit you so hard your heads all will spin!"

He swung with such force
that he fell from his ladder
right into the bin — and this made him madder!
With all of his wriggling and squirming around,
some of the grain poured out to the ground.

"My grain, oh, my grain!"
he snorted and sputtered.
"It can't be wasted — it can't," he muttered.
And then in a frenzy he looked all about
to see just how much of his grain had spilled out.

A poor man had started to pick up the wheat,
for his wife and six children had nothing to eat.

"Stop it, you thief,"
cried the rich man, alarmed,
and the poor man went running
for fear he'd be harmed.

The rich man saw all of the wheat that was spilt —
a new place for grain would have to be built.

"I'll tear down the old one," he said gleefully,
"and make bigger bins — how grand they will be!"

His slaves worked hard, his slaves worked long
to make the new bins big and strong.
The master from his platform high
surveyed their work with watchful eye.

And when the job was finally done,
the night had come, gone was the sun.
He hurried home all full of pride —
as full as the bins
with his grain inside.

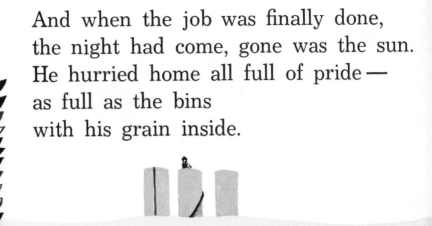

He went to his room and looked in the mirror.
He talked to himself, and he saw a good hearer.

"I really am a remarkable guy!
My riches will last till the day I die.

"I'll wear fine clothes
that are made of gold thread,
with gems on my belt, on my hands, on my head.
I'll eat and I'll drink, I'll dance and be gay,
and plan bigger things the rest of the day."

With a yawn and a stretch he turned to his bed.
"I'll think of my future tomorrow," he said.
Then looking once more at each wonderful bin,
he drew up the covers and tucked himself in.

The lamps on the bins
shone down through the night
to warn the rich man if thieves came in sight.
His treasure of grain was part of his plan
to be each day a much richer man.

"Someday," he said, "I'll start anew
and live as God would like me to.

But first things first — myself I'll please
and live my life in wealth and ease."

But that very night he died in his sleep,
with no one to mourn him and no one to weep.
This man had been selfish with all of his wheat;
he had offered no grain for the hungry to eat.

"How silly the rich, greedy man was!" you say.
Yes, he was silly, and right to this day,
because he was selfish and heartless and cruel,
he's not called the rich man —
he's called the rich fool.

Dear Parents:

The aim of our story isn't to create fear but to show how foolish it is to think the way this farmer did. It is important for us to understand and to help our children understand that Jesus isn't saying that we shall die if we are selfish but that it is senseless and foolish to think our belongings can insure us a happy life and future.

Our security lies in God. We are His children. He cares for us and provides what we need. Will you help your child to sense this in the way you teach him to look at life?

The Editor